Open to HOPE

Handling the Holidays After Loss

Dr. Gloria Horsley ♦ Dr. Heidi Horsley

And the Open to Hope Contributors

Foreword by Ann Hood,
New York Times bestselling author of
The Knitting Circle and *The Red Thread*

Open to Hope

Published by the
Open to Hope Foundation

Published by the Open to Hope Foundation
1485 Dana Avenue, Palo Alto, CA 94301

www.opentohope.com

Open to Hope Foundation helps people find hope after loss. The online forum at www.opentohope.com supports those who have experienced loss by helping them cope with their pain, heal their grief, and invest in their future. We encourage our visitors to read, listen, and share their stories of hope, love, and compassion.

ISBN: 978-0-9836399-1-6

Printed in the United States of America.

For our lost loved ones and all of us
trying to find peace during the holidays

If you would like to apply to write about grief, loss, hope, and healing for the Open to Hope Foundation, please go to www.opentohope.com and fill out the section under "Write for Us."

Table of Contents

Part 3: Finding Your Way Back to Christmas

Part 4:
Embracing the New Year with Hope

Foreword

Every year, as the cold season sets in, we inevitably find ourselves racing headlong into Thanksgiving and the holiday season. What knits together these busy, often festive weeks at the end of each year is the consistent thread that weaves in and out of all our lives: a sense of family.

Whatever family may mean for you, this is a time when we gather and reconnect with the ones we love. Maybe some of us have come in from out of town, out of the country, or simply across the street. We gather around the Thanksgiving table, light the menorah, or wonder what's under the Christmas tree, and generous servings of love and affection are served. Each year, we come together in a new way.

When you lose someone you love and that deeply cherished circle is broken, however, just facing the inevitability of the next hour, let alone weeks and weeks of festivities, conviviality, and social obligations, can feel unbearable.

After our 5-year-old daughter, Grace, died in 2002 of a viral infection, my family was shattered. The word "heartbroken" does not begin to describe our loss. At first, I couldn't read. I was a professional writer who could no longer write. It took me two years to reenter her room. The holidays were just not on my radar, though I tried hard to muster the energy for my son, Sam, and my husband.

The first year, we mourned for Grace and the loss of her presence in our lives. The second year, we grieved for ourselves because we knew she would never again come bounding down the stairs in her jammies to see what Santa had brought. By year three, we'd begun to move out of the fog, and glimmers of hope, like shoots of new grass, began to surface.

In came Annabelle, the little girl we adopted from China. I like to say that she was in need of a family and our family was in need of a child, so it was a perfect fit for all of us. While Annabelle could never replace Grace, nor would we want her to, she has brought our family so much love and has given Sam another sister. This year, I'm looking forward to hearing Annabelle's laughter and joy as she opens her presents on Christmas morning.

This is my journey, but, as you know, there are many journeys through the grief. This holiday season, you may be grieving a fresh wound to your heart. Or your ache may be longstanding, and perhaps softer and less biting. Whatever the case, you'll find comfort and practical advice in these pages.

Open to Hope: Handling the Holidays After Loss is a survival guide. These wonderful, insightful writers, all contributors to the Open to Hope Foundation's website, are sharing their most intimate stories of grief, longing, and resilience with one goal in mind: to show you and others who reluctantly stand in the same awful pair of shoes that there is a path through the turkey leftovers, the trail of crumpled Christmas wrapping paper, and the tears to a new and hopeful future.

Yes, the holidays will be different now, but love never dies. The love and memories that you have for that special person will continue to grow as the sadness is replaced with the joy of the celebration of life.

So as you read through these stories and suggestions, look for what fits you and your family, what feels useful, what brings you comfort. And also look for those glimmers of hope in your horizon. They are there, just waiting to be found.

I wish you and yours the best during this holiday season.

—Ann Hood

Acknowledgments

As with our first book written with the Open to Hope contributors, *Open to Hope: Inspirational Stories of Healing After Loss*, a book like this comes together only through the dedication and selfless sharing of talent and energy from many, many people. Thanks to each of our Open to Hope authors, who have generously shared more than 2,500 wonderful stories and articles on www.opentohope.com. It was very challenging to select those who appear in this book. Thanks to Neil Chethik, our website's executive editor, and Heather Johnson, our Open to Hope Community Manager, for bringing these messages of care, healing, and hope together so seamlessly on our website.

Thanks to Stephanie Abarbanel for her tremendous editing efforts. Thanks, too, to Beverly McManus and Karen Lau for organizing and helping shape the book, to Karla Wheeler and the team at Quality of Life Publishing for their design and production support, and to Todd Perkins and everyone at AlphaGraphics for providing layout, printing, and fulfillment. A special appreciation to Ann Hood for writing the book's foreword. We so appreciate the support of our spouses and families, and of course, we are grateful for our loved ones who have gone before us and who inspired each of us to do this work and to share their stories.

Introduction

We know the holidays can be a difficult time for you and your family after losing someone you love. Heidi and I—and our entire family—remember well the first holiday season after our 17-year-old son and brother, Scott, was killed in a car accident along with his 17-year-old cousin, Matthew.

That first year was particularly challenging. We found that as individuals and family members we did not always agree on how—or even *if*—we wanted to celebrate Thanksgiving and Christmas. Over time, we have developed our own personal and collective ways of acknowledging our loss and yet also remembering the good times during the holiday season.

Receiving advice, support, and encouragement from those already on this grief journey made all the difference for us. Their insights helped get us to the point where we again looked forward to the holidays. And, perhaps most importantly, little by little our hearts began to open to hope.

That's why we are so eager to share with you these heartfelt stories and articles contributed by the wonderful writers at our Open to Hope Foundation. We created Open to Hope in 2008 to provide interactive forums with a simple mission: Helping people find hope after loss. Our goal was to provide an open platform for individuals, grief experts, and organizations to serve the grieving public with a combination of expert articles, news research, radio, video, and, perhaps most of all, solace to those who are feeling the ache and anguish of losing a loved one.

In these pages, you will find wonderful presents for the holidays: The gifts of understanding, hope, and advice that will carry you through the hectic days ahead, filled with social gatherings, shopping, and holiday cheer you may not be feeling. When (and how) do you say, "No"? And when do you say, "Yes"? Is it okay to feel and celebrate the joy of the moment? Or, does that make you somehow disloyal to the memory of the one you've lost? Which family traditions do you keep and which are just too painful?

Many others have navigated these confusing, anxiety-producing, and, yes, potentially tearful moments. Let them guide you through to a happier and more productive New Year. They have been there before you and made it, and you can, too.

You need not walk alone during this or any other holiday season. And, as always, if you have lost hope, Heidi and I invite you to *lean on our hope until you again find your own.*

—Dr. Gloria Horsley and Dr. Heidi Horsley

PART 1

Rethinking Holiday Traditions

"Happy" Holidays? Not for the Newly Bereaved

By Karla Wheeler

This holiday season, an estimated one in 20 Americans will be grieving the loss of someone dear. And for some bereaved folks, the loss is so profound in their lives that they shudder at the thought of celebrating anything, especially a season that is supposed to be merry and jolly.

If you are dreading the upcoming holiday season because your loved one has died, please take a deep breath. Help is on the way. Know that your feelings are normal and there are a number of things you can do to ensure you and your family will get through the holidays in a loving, comforting, meaningful way. Here are some suggestions:

Choose rituals wisely

First, decide which family rituals and customs feel right and which ones seem too painful. For instance, if the thought of engaging in all the traditional activities you've done for years seems too stressful, give yourself and your family permission to spend Christmas or Hanukah at the home of relatives or close friends. This may mean you drive across town or hop on a plane to a faraway destination. No matter. Just be sure to choose wisely.

You'll want to spend this first holiday with those who have been totally supportive of your grief journey—people who let you grieve in your own unique ways and on your own individual timetables. Don't hesitate to invite yourselves over. They will understand and be grateful that you reached out to them, allowing them to nurture you during the most bittersweet holiday season you've ever experienced. Or, if you decide to stay home, consider inviting over relatives, neighbors, or friends whose company you truly welcome right now. Their hugs and camaraderie will help shift the energy in your home from loss to enduring love.

Avoid the word "should"

In your own self-talk, be gentle with yourself. Most importantly, avoid using "should." There are no "shoulds" when it comes to grieving, especially during the busy holiday season. This time of year can be the most difficult, triggering intense emotions for those who mourn. Instead of thinking, "I really should mail out my usual hundred holiday greeting cards," say to yourself, "If I find the time and my heart is healed enough, I might send out some greeting cards." Quite simply, just change any "I should…" phrases to something much less demanding of yourself, such as, "If I have time, I might…"

Give gifts for your loved ones

Since he or she isn't here to buy gifts for, decide as a family what charity you would like to support in his or her memory. For example, if Dad was an animal lover, you might choose the local animal shelter or humane society. You, the kids, and grandkids can go on a shopping spree to purchase items you know dogs and cats would love. Then plan a visit to the shelter where you can brighten the holidays for abandoned or orphaned pets. Or if Dad was a veteran of the Armed Forces, you may purchase toys to donate to local bereaved families who have lost a loved one on active duty overseas. After you share your gifts with those in need, take time to talk with each other about Dad and the ways he enriched the lives of others.

Acknowledge the empty chair

At the holiday dinner table, whether you are at home or visiting others, arrange for a place to be set for Dad, or whoever is missing. Everyone is feeling the impact of the empty chair, so why not take time to acknowledge this loss? While dinner is being prepared, ask each person to write down a fond memory of him. For young children, ask them to think about Dad and draw a picture. Place the writings/drawings on the table, next to each person's plate. Once everyone is seated, take a few minutes to ask each person to read or display his or her special sentiment. The love notes can then be placed onto Dad's dinner plate, helping to fill the void of the empty chair as you rekindle your love for your loved one—and for each other.

Attend grief support meetings

If the emotional trauma of your loved one's death seems too much to bear for you or any family member this holiday season, consider attending grief support meetings. Most hospices nationwide offer free bereavement meetings during afternoons and evenings to anyone in the community who needs counseling. You can find a local hospice by visiting the National Hospice and Palliative Care Organization website at www.nhpco.org.

Receive the joy

It's okay to be happy and joyful during the holiday season, even when our hearts are aching with sadness. When we're mourning, we sometimes feel guilty about laughing and having a good time. So give yourself—and your family—permission to experience those moments of joy. In so doing, you will be honoring the memory of your loved one in beautiful ways.

Karla Wheeler has been an expert in hospice care and grief support for more than 20 years. A former newspaper reporter and editor, she is the founder of Quality of Life Publishing Company, dedicated to helping hospices provide compassionate care worldwide. Five members of Karla's immediate family have experienced a "good death," thanks to hospice, including her 54-year-old husband. She is the author of several gentle grief support books and is a Board Member of the Open to Hope Foundation. Find more at www.opentohope.com.

"I'm Not Ready Yet!"

By Darcie D. Sims, PhD, CHT, CT, GMS

We should know better by now. They shouldn't keep surprising us, but they do. No matter how hard we try, no matter what we do to prepare ourselves, they still happen. Year after year, generation after generation, they arrive without hesitation or delay. They stay too long and never last long enough. They are filled with great anticipation and dread, and we never learn enough and we know far too much. The holidays are coming, and they're always ushered in by the universal cry, *"I'm not ready yet!"*

I haven't even cleaned up the fireworks from the Fourth of July. I'm still unpacking boxes (we've moved....again!), and the calendar says it's time for the "Great Stuff the Turkey" contest (the turkey won last year). Because we're in another new home, there will be the dilemma of where to put the Christmas tree and how to explain that one empty stocking to visitors.

I can't find the ornaments and keep forgetting where I've hidden the gifts I bought during the summer. We'll have to figure out where to hang a wreath and whether we should go with electric lights in the yard this year. Nothing seems to fit in this place like it did in the last one!

We always seem to have been more comfortable in the last place we lived. At least we knew where the memories were and how to handle them. Here, in this new place, no one knows *our story*. No one knows our history. It is as if we have no past. It's easy to blend in, but not so easy to settle in. And now the holidays are coming.

We all feel this way sometimes. *"I'm not ready yet!"* for first grade, for crossing the street by myself, for sleepaway camp, for junior high, for getting married, for getting a job, for having children, for burying someone I love. *"I'm not ready yet!"* to grieve, for living where no one knows my story.

"I'm not ready yet!" for the annual flood of memories that always spill out as we unpack the stockings from their tissue-wrapped nest. Or for the clutch of pain that still wraps my heart in grief as we place the ornaments on the tree. *"I'm not ready yet!"* to welcome in strangers who are fast becoming friends but who may never know the effort it has taken to be who I am now.

"I'm not ready yet!" to be normal. We look normal, and for the most part we act normal. We are normal, except for *our story* and for the tears in our family fabric. But no one knows about those tears anymore, and I don't think I'm ready not to have a past just yet. I don't think I'm ready for no one to remember our hurt, let alone the joy our loved ones gave us.

I unpacked the silver today, intending to polish it and place it in the dining room to add shimmer to the festive decorations. As I traced my fingers over the delicately carved designs in the coffeepot, I remembered my mother patiently teaching me how to polish good silver. I wasn't ready for the loneliness that swept over me as I placed the teapot on the tray and suddenly wanted to call Mom to tell her that I was, at last and again, home. She had taught me that silver always spoke of a comforting home, and now that I had set it out, I wanted someone to remember with me.

"I'm not ready yet!" to live only on the surface of life. I want to share my history with my new friends, yet it seems unfair to spoil their holiday season. It's not the same for me. There is still a lot of empty in my heart.

It doesn't matter whether you have moved or lived in the same place for generations, you still get an unsettled feeling the first time no one remembers the journey you've been on. The first time no one mentions *the name,* a hollowness leaves us empty and feeling alone. It is as if most of the world has forgotten the price we paid for this "new normal."

As long as we have the stockings up and the silver polished, let the holidays come! We'll gather together and count our blessings, not only naming the ones around the table, but also including those whose lives have touched ours in countless ways. One does not have to be present to be alive in our hearts. The heart never forgets, even when the world does.

No, nothing fits this year, just like nothing fit last year or the year before. But it's getting better, improving either with age or experience or patience. Or maybe it is simply becoming a thread in the continuing fabric of our lives. We will probably always be a bit unsettled and unnerved when the roll call finds a name missing or a chair empty. But then, why shouldn't we be a little sad when a light goes out in our world?

So, this holiday season, gather in your blessings and count them all. Count the blessings of the people in *your story,* and find the peace that comes with a holiday of joy remembered and love shared.

Peace to us all—wherever we may be.

Darcie D. Sims, PhD, CHT, CT, GMS, is a bereaved parent and child, a grief management specialist, a certified thanatologist, a certified pastoral bereavement specialist, and a licensed psychotherapist and hypnotherapist. She is the author of *Why Are the Casseroles Always Tuna?* as well as eight other books, DVDs, and CDs. Darcie is president of GRIEF, Inc., a grief consulting business, and director of The American Grief Academy® in Seattle. She is also the director of training for the Tragedy Assistance Program for Survivors. Read other articles by Darcie on www.opentohope.com.

Overcoming Depression During the Holidays

By Joan Horsley Haskins, BS, MSW, CSW

As Santa's "ho ho ho" drifts toward us, it may not sound too jolly if we are feeling sad. We tend to think everyone but us is happy, which is one of the biggest myths surrounding Christmas. According to statistics, there is a 15 percent increase in the number of individuals seeking help for emotional disorders in December.

Some causes of holiday depression are:

- Enormous pressure to get too much done within a specified time
- Overwhelming financial obligations, and worry about the bills you have accrued
- Relationships with family and friends, which are more complex and strained at a time when you want them to be perfect
- A schedule that is too demanding and leaves you unable to cope
- Fantasizing about a perfect Christmas and feeling

incapable of making it happen

- Family members who fail to cooperate with your carefully laid plans
- Worry that children may be disappointed with the gifts they receive or are too hyperactive or exhausted to respond in a loving manner
- Remembering past Christmases when life seemed better
- Mourning the loss of a loved one through death, divorce, or separation
- The feeling that if you can't be happy at Christmas, you may never be happy again

What can you do to overcome holiday depression?

- Stop putting unreasonable pressure on yourself to be happy. Acknowledge the reasons you are sad.
- Realize that, in spite of appearances, most of us are no more or less happy at Christmas than at other times of the year.
- Seek out the company of those who don't put demands on you to feel better than you really do.
- Be physically active. Exercise stimulates the production of endorphins, which are mood-elevating chemicals. Walk, go to a gym, or try aerobics.
- Set one or two simple tasks to do daily and complete them. Plan well ahead of each event to avoid last-minute panic.
- Realize that Christmas blues are usually temporary

- Get together with others and tell them what you fear the most about holidays. Saying things out loud makes them easier to cope with.
- Make a budget and stick to it.
- Don't overprogram yourself or your family. Include in your plans only the things that bring the most satisfaction and share the responsibility of preparations with others.
- Don't let the media's emphasis on family togetherness make you feel like you're the only one who is lonely and sad. Reach out to others, even if it's a conversation in the post office or grocery store.
- Join the church choir.
- If you know you'll be alone, don't isolate yourself. Invite someone to join you or plan to do fun activities by yourself that you normally don't have time to do. Your energy level increases when you're happy.
- Plan ahead for post-holiday depression and organize some unusual activities. Look forward to doing them.
- Don't expect the celebration to be perfect—nothing ever is. Don't dwell on regrets, such as, "It would have been so great if..."
- Praise yourself for your success and forget the failures. Realize that we all have a limited amount of energy and we are not responsible for everyone else's happiness.
- Be aware that, at times, even if you're surrounded by loved ones and things are going well, you may still

feel a hollow emptiness inside that can't be explained. Perhaps this is an unconscious fear of what the future holds.

- Buy yourself one irresistible gift so that if the things you receive are less than wonderful, you'll still feel satisfied.
- Don't compare this year's celebration with those in the past. Each holiday has its own highs and lows.
- Find joy in the simple things of daily life and contentment within yourself. You can choose to think depressing thoughts or ones that are uplifting. It is up to you.
- Do some volunteer work. You are needed and will meet some fascinating people.
- Don't have expectations that others in your life will lift you out of your depression, or even notice that you're blue, unless you tell them.

It may take years to ease the sadness of a loved one's death, and the sorrow is intensified at Christmas, especially if the deceased was a child. You can find help through support groups such as The Compassionate Friends. This organization offers solace to those who have lost children through accidents, illnesses, suicides, or stillbirths.

No matter what has been the source of your pain, keep telling yourself that you are not alone and that there are others experiencing the same feelings you are. But if your holiday lows become severe or prolonged, and you feel consumed by hopelessness and despair, you need to be concerned about chronic depression.

If this seems to be the case, please seek professional help. Here are some symptoms to be watchful for: Things that used to bring pleasure have lost their joy. You may experience sleep difficulties, lose your appetite for food, be disinterested in sex, or have trouble concentrating or accomplishing even simple tasks.

Before depression overwhelms you, look under Mental Health Associations in the yellow pages for a therapist or ask your clergy-person or family doctor. In many facilities, the cost is based on your ability to pay. A combination of therapy, exercise, and medication can knock out almost any depressive episode.

Don't delay seeking treatment. The longer your depression is allowed to consume you, the more difficult it will be to overcome. Be aware, too, of subtle changes and "downs" in family members and friends. Your encouragement can mean a lot if someone is suffering. There is help available—even during the holidays—and you can be the one to suggest treatment. Do so with love and concern, never diminishing another's feelings.

Joan Horsley Haskins, BS, MSW, CSW, lives in Salt Lake City, Utah, and has four children and eight grandchildren. This article holds special meaning for Joan this Christmas because her husband, Richard, a pioneer in pediatric dentistry, died several months ago. She is the author of *The Miracle of the Ivy: A True Tale of Comfort for Times of Loss*. Joan writes for the *Kern County Family Magazine* and for "Kids' Reading Room" at the *Los Angeles Times*. She is a time management and organization consultant and has her own non-profit organization, Greatest Gift, to help prevent child abuse. Read more at www.opentohope.com.

Making It Through the Season

By Barb Roberts

This may be your first or second holiday without your loved one. How do you get through this huge wave, this tsunami, looming before you? How do you cope when every time you turn on the television or go to the market, you see those around you with an intact family, with a holiday smile, and you feel like you are literally crumbling inside?

There is no right or wrong way to respond when grieving—particularly grieving through the holiday season. We, and sometimes those in our lives, have the erroneous notion that we are all going to grieve just like someone else. Each family member, each widow or widower, each child, each parent, each grandchild, each grandparent, and each friend grieves as an individual. Though we are not alone on our journey, it is definitely an individual journey.

I also want to remind you that *grief takes as long as it takes!*

Not *all* of the following suggestions will be right for you. Just as grief is an individual journey, grief help is also individual. There are very few "shoulds" here. Some of you agonized through a slow, painful death with your loved one; for others, it was sudden and traumatic.

You may wish that you could go to sleep and wake up on January 2, when the holidays are a memory and the New Year has begun. Then, there may be others who are afraid of what the New Year will bring.

Here are some hints (in no particular order) about getting through the holidays when grief may be all you see:

- Do not keep silent. Find someone with whom you can let down your guard and express your grief. Find people who will let you cry freely or express your anger. Find a person you trust and are comfortable with to share your heart. Talk openly with other family members: "How in the world are we going to get through the holidays this year?" By voicing the question that they may be feeling as well, you have taken the proverbial elephant out of the living room and addressed your collective pain. Ask for and accept help for the holiday details—shopping, cooking, cleaning, baking, wrapping, and decorating.
- Do what brings genuine comfort, even if it seems odd to others.
- Keep the traditions that have the most meaning for you, but feel free to start new ones.
- Brace yourself for the wave effect. You'll be cooking a turkey, doing fine, congratulating yourself about how well you are getting through the day, when a whiff of pumpkin pie—or a favorite carol, color, or ornament—reminds you. It comes unexpectedly and can throw you! Allow yourself to "feel the feeling" of grief—even if it only lasts for a brief time. In those

moments, give yourself permission to grieve, cry, stare off into space, and remember. In fact, sometimes it is helpful to just allow the "flooding" to come. Find a quiet, safe place and give in to the tears. Having taken the time you need to do that, you may better be able to interact with your family and friends during other parts of the day.

- If you are religious, lean on your faith in our loving God. Jesus says, "Come to me all who are weary and burdened, and I will give you rest." God has promised to never leave us nor forsake us. Psalm 23 says, "Our Shepherd has said that He walks beside us through the valley of the shadow of death, tenderly caring for us as a shepherd cares for his sheep."
- Speak of your loved one whenever he or she comes to mind—no holding back for fear of depressing yourself or others, including no holding back the tears or expressions of sorrow that naturally flow. Do one special thing to commemorate how much you miss your loved one.

You may feel guilty for experiencing pleasure and joy during the holidays—that somehow you are being disloyal to your loved one. Instead, try to savor these joyous moments during the holiday season. A grieving family I know wrote that they intentionally gave more thought to each holiday task, from wrapping presents to mailing cards, appreciating them as time-honored rituals instead of dreary chores to be gotten out of the way.

Again, not all of these ideas will be right for everyone.

Barb Roberts has been in the ministry of Pastoral Care for 25 years, where, having experienced grief and loss in her own life, she has been privileged to help those who grieve. She is a conference speaker and teacher on the topic and published *Helping Those Who Hurt: A Handbook for Caring and Crisis,* including lists, step-by-step directions, scripture, and vignettes. Read her articles at www.opentohope.com.

Keeping the Holiday Blues at Bay

By Beverly Chantalle McManus

Throughout the months approaching the holidays, when the days grow shorter and nights fall ever earlier, I have learned that unless I actively strive to keep the holiday blues at bay, I can end up feeling quite depressed and find myself in a very dark place. Especially in the eight years since my husband, Steve, died, the holidays bring on a certain melancholy for me. Perhaps it's due in part to my own circadian rhythms, perhaps it's hormonal, perhaps it's all the "special dates" that occur in the fall—Steve's birthday at the end of October, the anniversary of our first date, and later, our engagement. Or it could be all the family get-togethers around Thanksgiving and Christmas, where his absence is so glaring.

In the early years after Steve died, not knowing what to expect made it particularly hard. I didn't know how I'd feel or how our daughters would react to the holidays without their Daddy there. Plus, the holidays bring back so many memories of our loved ones—good and bad. Every song, smell, and tradition can be bittersweet. And initially, joy can make us feel guilty. We worry that if we let go of the pain, we will let go of the memory of our spouse. It can feel disloyal to experience positive (or negative) feelings when we miss him so much.

Then there are the well-meaning people who tell us that our loved ones would want us to have a happy holiday. While we know this on an intellectual level, our hearts aren't ready to accept it.

When I was walking around with a broken heart, I felt even more like an outsider, like others didn't understand that our world had ended. This was especially true during the holidays, when everyone is supposed to "be of good cheer" and it seems that happiness abounds. It's taken a while for my heart to understand that Thanksgiving and Christmas will never be the same again. Knowing in advance what changes to expect does help keep the holiday blues at bay.

You may find yourself:

- Feeling numb, feeling the holidays are surreal, viewing everything through a gauze curtain, feeling disconnected, pasting on a smile, but crying inside, and going through the motions for the children and extended family
- Figuring out how to fill new roles (or deciding which ones to give up)—who's going to be Santa Claus this year? Bake the cookies? Hang the lights?
- Missing the loving intimacy that comes with the holidays: Waking up next to the empty pillow, planning alone, shopping alone, cooking alone, wrapping alone, and singing alone

During those early years without Steve, I had to rapidly learn to take control of my time and commitments. I decided I didn't need to be afraid to say "No," but also reminded myself to say "Yes." I also found it useful to remind myself that grief takes time and energy—and that I needed to plan for this so I wouldn't feel so blindsided. This meant setting aside time each day to be alone, to cry, to feel, and to remember. I tried to give up the strong ties to past traditions and rituals, and did only what I felt I could handle without getting stressed out.

I found that keeping the kids in the loop with these changes was very important. When Steve died, our daughters were 16 and 18 years old, and I knew I needed to find out what they wanted and had the energy to do before making any plans that included the entire family or would change our annual festivities.

Steve was such a Christmas guy and had always taken painstaking care to decorate our home with outdoor lights, carefully making sure each tree bough had sufficient tiny lights, and then he would decorate the entire house with an abundance of holiday décor. After he died, the girls and I couldn't bear the thought of opening up those Christmas ornaments and facing the flood of memories they would surely unleash. So we simply left them in the storage bins and bought new decorations.

In that first year, we chose a tiny silk tree, decorated exclusively with candy canes and other edible ornaments, so we wouldn't have to face the massive "let's put away the Christmas décor" chores after the holidays were over.

In many ways, the second year was harder than the first, because by that time, people had forgotten about the loss and expected that we were no longer grieving. For us, however, the numbness had finally worn off and we were faced with the grim pain of realizing, "Oh, so *this* is how it's going to be."

In the years that followed, I'd come a long way in the healing process, but the holidays could still bring unexpected storms of emotions and feelings. It was still important to carve out time to grieve. I realized that though others may have forgotten that the girls and I were still hurting, we still needed special care and consideration. I found that a gentle reminder was occasionally needed when others (especially family members) had unrealistic expectations about holiday plans that included us.

We all prefer to keep it simple. For example, we have simplified our gift-giving rituals, which, in the past with Steve, could be quite elaborate. Instead, we decided to use the funds and energy we would have spent on each other to benefit La Casa de las Madres, a shelter for abused women and children. We have had so much fun "helping Santa," and it has helped us get through the loneliness that the holidays seemed to highlight with Steve's absence.

I've also learned that it's a good idea to communicate early any changes in our holiday plans to all involved. For example, early on my daughters and I realized we just weren't up for the usual "all-family" Thanksgiving feasts that at times have included up to 50 of our cousins, aunts, and uncles. So for the past few years, we have instead enjoyed a small dinner at a favorite restaurant. One year, part of the family decided to forego the big feast and joined us at the restaurant instead.

Sometimes the seasonal blues still do creep up on me, especially when I'm engaged in a big work project that harnesses all my attention. Without even realizing what's happened, I'll suddenly notice that I am gradually finding myself more anxious, lonely, and stressed. I start to feel hollow and inadequate.

Over the years, I've learned a few strategies that help keep the blues at bay. If you find yourself descending into the seasonal blues, I invite you to try them and see what works for you.

What I've discovered:

- Take it one day at a time, or one hour at a time, or

even one minute at a time. Just remember: "It's only a day. I've already survived the worst. I can get through this."

- Let people know as early as possible of any changes in plans.
- Give yourself permission to have a good cry.
- If you have children, make sure they know it's okay to feel what they're feeling and to cry if they need to.
- Take a break and go for a walk. Spend time in nature to recharge your emotional batteries.
- Don't resort to alcohol or drugs to numb your pain. Enjoy the festivities, but don't overdo it.
- Don't be afraid to decline invitations. Practice saying, "Thanks for the invitation, but that's just not going to work for us this year."
- But also, make an effort to connect with others when you're up for it. Invite supportive friends or family to accompany you to events you wish to attend. But only invite those who support your healing journey, not those who are toxic and make you miserable.
- Begin a new ritual, perhaps leaving an empty chair and place setting at the table and lighting a candle in honor of that dear person who is not there with you in person.
- Remind everyone, including yourself, that grieving is a natural process. We hurt so much because we loved so much.
- When all else fails, try chocolate. Really! It helps our bodies release a cascade of "feel good" chemicals that

can help lift our spirits. Even if it's just a temporary fix, sometimes that's all we need to sidestep the full-blown onset of the holiday blues.

Most of all, I've learned that although things will never be the same, that doesn't mean that I can't experience joy once again. I've come to accept that it will be a different joy. I will never forget Steve and other loved ones who have died, because they will always be in my heart. I am thankful that, especially during the holidays, my memories will continue to connect me with those who have made me who I am today.

Beverly Chantalle McManus lives in Northern California with her two daughters, who have both now graduated from college. She is Vice President and Treasurer of the Board of the Open to Hope Foundation, a bereavement facilitator and core team member of the Stepping Stones on Your Grief Journey Workshops, and a frequent speaker and writer on the topic of loss and grief. In addition to grief support, she is also a marketing executive for professional services firms. Read her articles at www.opentohope.com.

PART 2

Gathering at Thanksgiving

Thanksgiving Day Can Be Painful

By Mary Jane Hurley Brant, MS, CGP

When you lose someone you love, Thanksgiving Day feels burdensome and painful. When a brain tumor took away our precious Katie's life, I dreaded that holiday. For seven years, we served no rutabagas because they were Katie's favorite vegetable. The thought of their seasonal aroma wafting through our home without her in it was too much to bear.

I don't share this part of me today to make you sad. I share it because you are my extended family and I am yours. We are all fellow travelers. When we suffer loss, we question if we will ever overcome the pain of its paralyzing grief.

We think we won't survive and doubt we can ever feel happy again. Even poor Charlie Brown had doubts. "I think I'm losing control of the whole world," he once said with a sigh. Giving thanks seems counterintuitive, too, when we only feel like crying. But we can give thanks, and we can go on. Here are a few suggestions on how to go about it:

- Make the conscious decision to live. That means you get out of bed every day and put your feet down on the floor. Say, "Thank you for my feet" even if they don't feel like walking.

- Allow yourself private time and space to quietly listen to songs that were important to your loved one and cry some more. Sigh some more. Then switch to a different kind of music to distract yourself.
- Do something active, such as taking a walk and meditating on your specific pain. Have a little talk with the beloved person you lost and allow your tears to flow. They are healing you.
- Write your longings for your beloved in a private journal. Expressing your feelings is crucial for your journey through grief and sorrow.
- If you don't feel like cooking Thanksgiving dinner, go to someone else's home or to a movie instead—normal has been redefined for you.
- If you have children or grandchildren, hug them. Children don't always understand death, but they understand life, and it will rub off, I promise.
- Turn toward your mate or friends for consolation, not against them.
- Remember, the stages of grief and loss—denial, anger, bargaining, depression, and acceptance—are particularly intensified during the Thanksgiving holiday, so consciously reflect more on your many blessings and less so on your sorrow and losses. Our Katie told me more than once that someone else always has it worse, and she was correct.
- Pray for the strength and courage to accept your life now, then pray some more. Meditate. Yes, I know it's hard. I am not speaking in the abstract here; I am

with you every step of the way.

- Consider all the other people in your life who love and depend on you. They need and want you there physically, emotionally, and spiritually this Thanksgiving, even if you are sad. Why? Because they love you and want to give you an extra hug. We all need those extra hugs when we are hurting.

My friends, the Creator has planted an abundance of love and mercy in your heart for your loss. And while, yes, we must surrender to the physical absence of our beloved, we also trust with all our soul that they are at peace now, and we will be given the grace to find peace, too, and the courage to make this Thanksgiving Day and every day matter.

Mary Jane Hurley Brant, MS, CGP, has been a practicing psychotherapist, who specializes in grief, for 31 years. She is the author of *When Every Day Matters: A Mother's Memoir of Love, Loss and Life*. In this first-person narrative, M.J. addresses the suicide of her father when she was 13 and the life and death of her daughter, Katie, who died of a brain tumor. She is the founder of Mothers Finding Meaning Again. Find more at www.opentohope.com.

Mom's Turkey Stuffing Still Rules

By Gloria Arenson, MFT, DCEP

Thanksgiving is my favorite holiday. It was my mom's, too. She was a wonderful cook. Her turkey stuffing was simple but memorable. In fact, my brother used to tease that he was going to make a stuffing sandwich with the leftovers the next day. I think he really did. It tasted even better on day two.

My mom died the day before Thanksgiving in 1979. Every year since then, Thanksgiving has been bittersweet for me. It is still my favorite holiday because of the family togetherness and the wonderful feast, but it reminds me of her death, too.

One of the wonderful ways we commemorate my mother's life is by making her special stuffing, which has become a family tradition. No matter how fancy the food, her simple recipe is reproduced and eaten with gusto. Over the years, my son has taken on the job of creating this dish, and he does it with love as he remembers his grandmother, too. Of course, my mother has been gone a very long time, and I no longer grieve, but it is comforting for me to think of her as we are gathered together. Her spirit is always in my heart and I recall how she bustled around, making sure that everyone was stuffed and happy.

Whenever I feel sad, I try to practice the advice of a wonderful teacher and author, Ken Keyes, who said, "To be upset over what I don't have is to waste what I do have." Ken was the personification of that sentiment. He was a quadriplegic who could only move one finger. Yet he radiated love and light, and inspired thousands of people.

When I feel carried away by negative feelings, such as loneliness, grief, or hurt, I talk to myself out loud and make a list of what is in my life right now that cheers me up. I usually start with the basics—being grateful that I have a bed to sleep in, a roof over my head, and money in my wallet. I keep listing until I realize that I also have people who love and appreciate me, and I still have loving memories of the ones who are no longer with me.

Perhaps, like me, you have lost someone who was also a great cook. You might honor him or her by making his or her special dish and sharing it with friends and relatives. With each bite, you can remember and thank that loved one. If you are still grieving, make your own list of what you can be thankful for at this time of year and see if your mood shifts to the brighter side of life.

Gloria Arenson, a Licensed Marriage and Family Therapist and Diplomate in Comprehensive Energy Psychology, is passionate about helping people using Emotional Freedom Techniques (EFT) to heal negative emotions and behaviors. Gloria is the author of the award-winning book *Five Simple Steps to Emotional Healing,* and other books and articles. She is in private practice in Southern California. Read more of Gloria's articles at www.opentohope.com.

At the Table, Say Their Names

By Tom Zuba

This Thanksgiving marks the 21st that I've lived through since the death of my 18-month-old daughter, Erin, in 1990; the 12th since my wife, Trici, died in 1999; and the 6th since my 13-year-old son, Rory, died in 2005.

One thing I know for sure is that I can't expect anyone to mention the name(s) of the people I love who have died. Expecting someone to say their names only brings me disappointment and pain because there is a good chance that the day will pass without it happening. At least that has been my experience more than once.

Believe it or not, it's *my job* to bring the people I love who have died into the family gathering, and sometimes that can be tough to do. At a time when many of us are feeling incredibly vulnerable and fragile, the last thing we want is rejection or indifference. So I've come up with a few concrete ways we can let family and friends gathered for the holidays know that it's okay (in fact, comforting) to talk about our deceased loved ones.

- You can provide the favorite dish of the person you love who has died for the holiday get-together. Talk about him or her before you pass it around!

- Pass around a favorite picture or two. Work the picture(s) into the dining table's centerpiece. Perhaps you even have a picture of your loved one with each person who will be sitting around the holiday table. Use these pictures as place cards, propping each photo up against a glass or setting it in the middle of the plate. What a great way to get people talking!
- Bring a favorite memento—a book, a poem, a watch, a piece of jewelry, or a toy—and share it after dinner, before dessert is served.
- Have your loved one's favorite music playing in the background. Tell everyone the story!

One of our biggest fears is that the people we love will be forgotten. When no one mentions their names, especially at family-centered events, the loneliness we already feel can be magnified. Try not to be caught off guard. Think ahead. Be proactive. What can you do to bring the person you love smack in the center of your Thanksgiving gathering?

Tom Zuba is a grief guide, author, and inspirational speaker. His 18-month-old daughter, Erin, died suddenly in 1990. His 43-year-old wife, Trici, died equally as suddenly on New Year's Day 1999, and his 13-year-old son, Rory, died from brain cancer in 2005. Tom and his son, Sean, are learning to live full, joy-filled lives, one day at a time. Tom has appeared on *The Oprah Winfrey Show*. For more, visit www.opentohope.com.

A Child's Insight Offers Meaning—And a Laugh

By Laura Klouzek

The smell of turkey and stuffing was in the air; there was noise from the grandkids playing and dishes being prepared in the kitchen. It was our first Thanksgiving since my son, Lucas, died in July. The previous Thanksgiving, we had all been together and had even taken a special family picture to put on our Christmas cards. Lucas's absence made the day dreary, despite the festive holiday atmosphere.

Dinner was on the table, and it was time for a prayer. I felt I couldn't express thanks this particular day, as my heart was so heavy. As I looked at the other members of the family, I knew I was not alone in my sorrow.

I started my prayer and thanked God for the blessing of our family, who had held onto each other so tightly through the past four months. We are an amazing source of joy and strength to each other. As I finished the prayer, burning tears were streaming down my cheeks. I did not want to ruin this day for everyone, but I wasn't sure I could make it through the meal without breaking down.

When I knew the tears were coming again, I got up from the table and went to the front door. I wanted to shed these tears alone because I missed my son. As I stood looking out the door, my precious 6-year-old granddaughter came beside me. "Nana, what is wrong?" she asked. "Are you missing Lucas?"

"Yes, Cassidy, my heart is broken, and I miss him very much."

"But Nana, your other son, Josh, is still alive."

Oh, the perception of a child! I agreed with her, and we all had a good chuckle at her complete honesty.

I knew the holidays to come would not be easy, but we would make it through together. I allowed myself time to be sad and mourn the absence of my child. Then, I forced myself to remember my other son, Josh, his three sisters and their families, and my husband, all of whom are still alive.

And I am still alive. I will continue to give thanks, to cry, to mourn, and to smile. And I will give thanks for the precious insight of a special child.

Laura Klouzek's son, Lucas, died in July 2008 after a short fight with cancer. His death and her journey through grief have prompted her to help others through her writing and speaking. Laura and her husband, who live in rural Missouri, are the parents of five children and the grandparents of eight. They also spent 12 years as foster parents. For more about Laura, visit www.opentohope.com.

PART 3

Finding Your Way Back to Christmas

From Sad to Silly: Frosty Saves the Day

By Michele Neff Hernandez

There is a song on the radio at this time of year, sung by the Carpenters, called "Merry Christmas, Darling." The first Christmas after my husband, Phil, died, hearing this song sent me into fits of tears. Not the sweet, sad, nostalgic type of tears. These were the hitting my hands on the dashboard or kicking my bed, angry, unreasonable type of tears.

Every time the song came on, I wanted to scream at the beautiful voice on the radio because the sentiment was so infuriating. The lyrics proclaim that every day is a holiday with the one you love, so even if you aren't together on Christmas Eve, no worries, you can be together in your dreams. At that point, I was way beyond wanting to spend Christmas with Phil in my dreams! What I wanted was to hold him, to feel his warm breath on my cheek, and to sit on the couch, side by side, sipping coffee while the kids opened their gifts on Christmas morning.

Every holiday tradition felt like a chore. Determined to check off each task on the list, I dutifully put up outdoor lights, crying yet again when I discovered how meticulously Phil had packed away the lights the year before. The kids and I dragged the tree into the house, but the glittering lights seemed to emphasize my gloominess.

Opening a storage box, I found old Christmas cards full of cheerful greetings and good wishes. I sighed out loud as I read each one, thinking how radically our lives had changed in only 365 days.

One evening, I reached into the bottom of the last plastic bin and pulled out Frosty. Phil was famous in our family for the dance he did when Frosty, who played "Rockin' Around the Christmas Tree" at the push of a button, made his holiday debut. Phil's dance included booty shaking, heel tapping, and all manner of silliness, which unfailingly created gales of laughter throughout the house.

No one could look at Frosty without giggling, because Phil's dance was so outrageous. The kids would even try to get him to perform for their friends, and they were always thrilled when he was successfully talked into a crowd-pleasing dance recital.

Sitting alone in front of the Frosty box, I was surrounded by my sorrow and filled with self-pity. All the things I missed most about my husband were represented by that stupid box—his love of life, his adoration of silliness, his ability to be completely in the moment, and his constant attempts to keep me laughing. My world was so empty and joyless without him.

While I sat contemplating how awful my life had become since Phil's death, I absently reached over and pushed Frosty's button. Even through my tears, I could not suppress the smile that Frosty's song brought to my face. It was as if Phil was standing right in front of me, in all his holiday glory, telling me to wipe away my tears and accept the joy the holiday season still offered.

Spontaneously, I recreated my husband's holiday jig. That night, Phil and I danced together, right in the middle of the kitchen. I could see his big smile and feel the warmth of his love with every note the silly toy snowman warbled. Plopping down in my seat at the end of the song—breathless and a little surprised—I felt a glimmer of joy for the first time in months.

The next time "Merry Christmas, Darling" came on the radio, I knew I needed to make peace with my inner Scrooge. As the opening chords played, I sat quietly and really listened. This time I heard a new message: Phil and I can no longer physically share the same couch on Christmas morning, but the memory of the many precious moments we shared over the years is mine forever.

In the years since his death, I have come to realize that I can have Christmas with Phil in my dreams for the rest of my life. There are still days when my heart aches with the need to feel his touch, and I often find the holidays to be bittersweet. Nonetheless, whenever I feel my despair growing, I counter it with a holiday jig and the love of the man who can still make me smile.

Michele Neff Hernandez's husband died in 2005. Since then, she has reached out to other widowed people as the founder and executive director of the Soaring Spirits Loss Foundation, which provides peer-based grief support programming worldwide. Michele is the creator of the Camp Widow program, a motivational speaker, freelance writer, and proud mom to three amazing kids. Read more of her articles at www.opentohope.com.

When Canceling a Holiday Is Not an Option

By Coralease Ruff, PhD, RN

In a flash, a heart-wrenching telephone call plunged my family and me into the ranks of the bereaved. The shock and excruciating pain was like nothing I'd ever felt before. Our beloved 21-year-old daughter, Kandy, was dead. I thought the pain would never stop.

Holidays, especially Christmas, are traditional family gatherings with lots of festivities. It begins after Thanksgiving and lasts forever, it seems. After suffering through that first Easter without my daughter, the first Mother's Day, her birthday, my birthday, and all of the other special days, I knew Christmas would be unbearable. I didn't know how I could possibly get through it.

What do you do, when canceling Christmas is not an option? I wanted to keep the spirit of the season for the rest of the family, who would be coming home for the holiday. But I knew I could not pretend Christmas was business as usual, since my world had crumbled.

First, I decided to compromise, so I decorated our home

differently. I replaced the red lamppost bows with purple bows and streamed blue lights on the front shrubbery in lieu of the sparkling clear ones. This was consistent with my blue mood. I managed to put up our traditional Christmas tree. All the while, my tears were falling on the ornaments, especially those that Kandy had made as a child.

Preparing our usual home-style Christmas dinner was not something I was willing to consider. In fact, I could not bear the thought of spending Christmas at home, without Kandy. She loved Christmas and was always the life of the party. I knew I had to get out of town, so I made reservations for my husband, son, and me at a nearby resort. This allowed us to hide away until Christmas Eve and Christmas Day were over.

My Christmas gift to the family was a video of Kandy's life, made especially for the occasion by a friend. I showed it on Christmas morning, hoping it would help ease the hurt of Kandy's absence. None of us really saw it. We sat like three zombies, each in our own private hell. I did survive that dreaded first Christmas, even though the sunshine was gone from my life.

After trying, unsuccessfully, to cancel the second and third Christmases, I made a point of inviting someone new to join us for Christmas dinner. This helped to give me someone different to focus on and a reason to prepare for the holiday. I also made a point of reaching out to others, through financial contributions to charities such as the Salvation Army and Toys for Tots in memory of our daughter. I also purchased holiday floral arrangements at our local church in her memory.

One bereaved mom from The Compassionate Friends provided an annual Christmas party complete with a clown, a Santa, and gifts for all the children at a local children's hospital, in memory of her daughter. Other grieving individuals say they serve meals at soup kitchens and homeless shelters.

I also bring my daughter's spirit into the yuletide season by participating in The Compassionate Friends Worldwide Candle Lighting, which takes place every second Sunday in December. All of these activities were helpful for me. In retrospect, it has been doing something different, reaching out to others, and establishing new traditions that have helped make the season more bearable and lessen the feelings of loss.

Now, nearly 14 years since the sudden death of our beloved daughter, I still feel the pain of her absence, especially at Christmas. However, the season no longer holds the same feelings of dread, even though life without her is forever changed. She is forever in my heart.

Coralease Ruff, PhD, RN, is a Bereavement Facilitator, a registered nurse, a university professor, and a former Board Member of The Compassionate Friends. She and her husband became bereaved parents in 1997, when their 21-year-old daughter died in a car accident in the Dominican Republic. Coralease is a frequent presenter on grief topics locally and nationally. She is an end-of-life nursing educator and has been published widely in professional nursing literature and the lay press. She is the author of *Her Light Still Shines*. Find more at www.opentohope.com.

The Date Always Catches Up with Me

By Scott Mastley

I believe, maybe because it helps me heal, that my brother, Chris, would want me to enjoy the holidays. His car accident was in December almost 15 years ago, and that December date catches up with me each year. I start to hide from the world around mid-November. I want to sleep more. I blink back tears watching sappy commercials. I don't feel like working or working out at the gym.

It happens right on cue every year, but it took me several years to realize the cause. I just thought it was holiday stress. Now I recognize it right away and know that I'm subconsciously dreading the December 5 angel date. The depression rolls in as if on cue.

When I didn't realize the cause of the depression, I let it roll over me and tried to keep it to myself. I didn't want to be a complainer. I thought about Chris every day, so I didn't see how this time of year was different.

Now I know it's going to happen, know why it's happening, and I've told my family about it. My wife knows that December can be a little crazy. It took me years to get excited about Christmas again after Chris's accident, but now I love it like I did before. It's the only time of year that I actually enjoy going to the mall.

Believing that Chris would want me to enjoy the holidays helped tremendously. I'm still going to cry when I see a sappy commercial, because the emotions are running high this time of year, but I'm also going to appreciate the holiday atmosphere.

In the early years, I tried distraction (going to the movies), escape (traveling to another town), and denial (pretending everything was okay). Distraction and escape were helpful at the time, but denial never worked.

Now I focus on my family. When I think about the hole that is Chris's absence, I look at other families. That's why I enjoy the mall at Christmas. It's packed with families—panicked parents and excited kids. I love to think that they are not burdened by anything as heavy as a lost sibling or child. They're just getting ready for another great Christmas. It helps me get ready for my own.

Scott Mastley's brother died in a car accident. To learn how to heal from his grief, he joined The Compassionate Friends and attended, and later led, the monthly sibling group meetings. He eventually was asked to be the Sibling Representative for metro Atlanta, which led to television appearances and his decision to write the book *Surviving a Sibling* to raise awareness about sibling loss. Read more at www.opentohope.com.

I Used to Love the Holidays

By Mary Rondeau Westra

The unease creeps in around Halloween. The orange and black décor, the miniature candies, the goblins at the door. It's just not as much fun as it used to be . . . when my son, Peter, was alive. When he was little, dressed as a baby blue rabbit, he took the hand of his older sister, dressed in her pink pajama sleeper, and they headed out with my husband with homemade ears on their caps.

I used to love the holidays . . . when Peter was alive. I used to be very well organized. I'd make a schedule for shopping, frosting cookies, and assembling gingerbread houses. We'd put up a big tree, entertain friends, and send holiday photo cards of our family of five.

Then, in July 2001, the holidays changed forever. It was just after the Fourth of July when the sheriff rang the doorbell and told us that our baby blue bunny, who'd become a strapping, handsome 24-year-old, had been kicked to death by bouncers outside a club in Atlantic City. Though we already had the perfect photo for that year's holiday card, we would not send it. Getting through the holidays would become a challenge.

At first, it hurt even to go into retail stores. I hated the decorations, and I couldn't stand to walk through the men's department and see clothes I couldn't buy for my son, or hear holiday music we wouldn't share. I would have preferred to skip the holidays, but my two daughters were coming home and they wanted the holidays to be "as normal as possible." So my husband and I got a small tree and left it bare for days.

I remembered seeing among Peter's boxes the basket of ornaments I'd sent him at college, mostly Santas on skis because skiing was his favorite sport. I dug out that box, and we hung Peter's ornaments on one side of the tree. Then we waited for the girls to help us finish.

In the years since Peter's death, we've tried different ways to get through the season. Sometimes we go away. Sometimes we go to parties, especially if they're small, or sometimes we decline. At times, we've entertained, but not as often as we used to. Our idea of fun has changed. We want to be with people we really care about. And most New Year's Eves, we're home together alone, for that has proven to be even more difficult than Christmas for my husband—all those dashed hopes. It's no longer an evening to party.

New rituals help keep Peter alive in spirit. I set up a little artificial tree in his room, one he used to have as a kid, and I decorate it with the little Santas. I hang his stocking on the mantel with the other stockings, though I always sit down afterward and ponder it for a moment. For Christmas dinner, we sometimes make sweet potatoes with marshmallows and pecans, just as Peter used to make them. I set the table with candles at each place, and we take turns going around the table sharing a memory. We talk about Peter. We laugh. We feel sad. We will always miss him.

Just before Christmas, half a dozen families who have lost children get together at our church to remember. We bring pictures and candles, and take turns talking about our special angels. Sometimes our surviving children participate. This sacred time, set aside during the busiest days, helps us honor our deceased children so that we can better focus on our surviving children for the remainder of the holidays.

I feel better when I try to be helpful. One year, we participated in Habitat for Humanity on the Saturday before Christmas. Our labor and the concern for the family who lived in that house took the spotlight off our own sadness. At Thanksgiving, I've helped prepare meals for families in need. Often, I get together with other mothers more recently bereaved than I, giving them a shoulder and an ear. I've found that helping others takes my mind off myself.

The holidays, I've learned, are not about me or my family or Peter. His absence will always be most poignant when we are all together. But there is truth in the cliché—which used to upset me in the days when I could think of nothing but his absence—that Peter would want us to be happy. He'd want us to think about others. I'm grateful people need me. Remembering my daughters, friends, and neighbors, and those who don't have Thanksgiving dinners, and doing what I can to help, honors Peter and keeps his spirit alive in my heart.

The holidays are about this enduring human spirit. It's a season to give thanks, to pray for peace, to love others, and to give way to hope for the future. It is a time to be selfless. Then, after all, the holidays are not so bad.

Mary Rondeau Westra is the author of *After the Murder of My Son*. A former teacher and fundraiser for arts organizations, she started journaling after her 24-year-old son's tragic death in 2001—writing to understand her feelings and putting them on paper so she didn't have to carry them in her heart. She gave a keynote address at the 2011 national conference of The Compassionate Friends. Mary and her husband, Mark, live in White Bear Lake, MN. Find more articles by Mary at www.opentohope.com

Rediscovering the Joy of Christmas

By Emily McManus

One of my family's most treasured Christmas Eve traditions was my father reading aloud *The Polar Express*, by Chris Van Allsburg, to my younger sister, my mom, and me. The story is about a young boy who travels to the North Pole where he meets Santa Claus and receives a bell that can only be heard by those who still believe in the magic of Christmas. Although he seldom cried, Daddy would tear up each year as he finished the story, which concludes, "At one time most of my friends could hear the bell, but as years passed, it fell silent for all of them. Even Sarah found one Christmas that she could no longer hear its sweet sound. Though I've grown old, the bell still rings for me as it does for all who truly believe."

I think my father always heard the bell.

My dad was diagnosed with esophageal cancer in the summer of 2002 when my sister was 16 and I was 18 years old. Following months of chemotherapy and radiation, the doctors performed surgery, and we discovered that the cancer had spread to other organs and was impossible to remove. He arrived home from the hospital at 9 P.M. on Christmas Eve, and although we did not know then that he would die the following February, that last Christmas was bittersweet, with many tears shed as we experienced Christmas together for the last time.

Christmas brought out the best in our family. Our dad loved playing Santa and was *almost* more excited about finding and giving the perfect gifts than we were to receive them. In our teenage years, he would wake us up bright and early, because he couldn't wait any longer for us to see what Santa had brought. From my earliest memories, my sister and I would wait in the hallway in our pajamas with our mom as Daddy would get the camera ready to capture our expressions. After my dad died, although the house was full of decorations and gifts, it still felt very empty.

For five years after my dad's death, I dreaded Christmas and would do my best to avoid or not participate in my family's rituals. Christmas reminded me of these lyrics from a song by Dar Williams, "And it felt like a winter machine that you go through and then you catch your breath and winter starts again, and everyone else is spring bound."

Winter is a time when the earth draws inward, when shorter hours of daylight invite us to insulate ourselves from the frigid outdoors. These urges to cocoon, and perhaps isolate, are familiar to those of us in grief. The holidays felt very dark, and I found it difficult to perceive any source of light, even as my mom worked very hard to maintain a sense of joy and continuity from our past Christmases. If I could have stayed in my college dorm by myself, I probably would have.

One year after my father's death, I tried to convince my mom and sister to skip Christmas altogether and spent most of the day alone. Other years, I became so stressed out in the lead-up to Christmas that I became sick by the actual day, in bed with the flu. During those years, I yearned for the past, thinking that if Christmas couldn't be as it once was, I didn't want to celebrate at all. In many ways, I thought that there was nothing left to celebrate.

The journey from childhood holiday seasons, full of fun, through the Christmases surrounding the death of my father to the present has been a journey from light through darkness to light again, like fall to winter and blossoming to spring. A spark of the Christmas spirit remained as we watched old home movies, kept traditions alive like singing lots of Christmas carols, and read stories aloud on Christmas Eve. That spark was kindled through slowly reincorporating favorite traditions, as well as creating new ones.

This past year was the first time since my dad died that I truly enjoyed Christmas, and the shift occurred when I decided to focus on bringing light to others in my family, rather than focusing on the lack of light within myself.

I will always think of my dad on Christmas. But rather than focusing on his absence, I now try to remember his exuberance and share examples of his big-heartedness with others. For example, my dad used to love playing videogames with us, so it was fun this year when Santa brought a new set of videogames for the family, including new versions of old classics that my dad loved to play.

It's fitting that Jesus spoke the words, "It is more blessed to give than to receive" (Acts 20:35), for it is never more true than when celebrating His birth.

The light we hold as individuals—in the form of memories of past celebrations, of laughter and singing, in the gestures of the loved one who has died, —transforms into warmth and love within the family. Just as the days become lighter and longer, we in grief slowly emerge from the cocoon that protected us at our most vulnerable moments.

It has been a long journey, but I am beginning to hear the bell again.

Emily McManus's father died of esophageal cancer when she was 18 years old. Emily earned her undergraduate degree from New York University. She has written and published original fiction and nonfiction; has edited numerous articles, journals, and books; and is an accomplished artist. While in college, she was an intern at *McSweeney's* and is currently attending graduate school. To read more articles like this, visit www.opentohope.com.

An Angel Tree and Roses for My Little Angel

By Amy Daly, MSW, LCSW, CT

"God gave us memories so we would have roses in December."
—James M. Barrie

By late 1998, I was preparing for my first holiday season without my precious daughter, Alexandria, who had died January 29, 1998, as a newborn. I had a 33-month-old son, Bryce. It had been almost a year since my daughter died, and I was halfway into the subsequent pregnancy with my third child, another girl. Surely I was through the worst of the grief, I thought.

I could not have been more wrong. By the grace of God, I made it through that first Christmas without my daughter. The day was miserable, though, a train wreck of sorts, when my emotions came out sideways.

That first Christmas, and my assumptions surrounding it, taught me important lessons about myself and my life after Alexandria: My life was not going to return to the normal I knew, I needed to be more gentle with myself, and most importantly, I needed to find a path in which I could honor my spiritual relationship with my daughter and find my own path with my grief. I vowed that the upcoming birthday, anniversary, and year of holidays were going to be different.

The second holiday season after Alexandria was born and died rolled around all too quickly. It was still painful, but, amidst the thorns, there were roses this time. I took the time to plan ahead and remember my daughter even in light of all the craziness of the season.

Bryce was almost 4 and Savannah, my rainbow baby, was 7 months old. It was a hectic time, to be sure. My stepmother gave me a small tabletop Christmas tree, and I found special angel lights to adorn it. By then, I had collected a number of angel ornaments that were gifts from family and friends, and other tokens I had purchased myself in memory of Alexandria.

I carefully decorated the tree. With each angel I hung, I remembered something special about my experience with my daughter—treasured moments when I was able to hold her, give her a bath, and see her smile. I still missed her terribly, but I was able to find some peace in my loving ritual.

This is the 14th December without my precious Alexandria. I will faithfully decorate the baby tree while quietly longing for her and, through the tears, remembering the special time I carried her safely inside me and the memories from the week we had together.

I will have roses in December.

Amy Daly, MSW, LCSW, CT, is a social worker and bereavement counselor. The death of her middle child, Alexandria Nicole Daly (1/22/98–1/29/98), was a life-changing experience. As a result of the loss, Amy returned to school and earned her master's degree in social work. In addition to the death of Alexandria, she lost her stepmother, Kathy Kuck Rowe, to cancer in June 2006. Amy lives in a suburb of Indianapolis with her husband and two children. Read more at www.opentohope.com.

Finding the "Christmas Valentine"

By Yvonne E. Lancaster

On December 22, 1986, our son, Brian, was killed by a drunk driver. We buried him two days later on Christmas Eve. Brian was 19 years old and a sophomore in college. All of his dreams and aspirations to become a marine biologist, and hopefully a husband and father someday, were dashed in a split second.

Brian's tragic accident was followed by intense grieving and mourning during the holiday season. Our world stood still; our lives were flash-frozen in time. Life would forever have two phases —life before Brian's death and life after Brian.

Brian was full of life and promise. He was a four-star athlete in high school and enjoyed being healthy, fit, and funny. Due to his easygoing nature, some people called him an old soul.

My husband, Tim, and I, along with our two surviving children, Elizabeth and Timmy, cancelled Christmas. The tree came down. The remainder of the gifts were never wrapped or opened. As we struggled with our sorrow over Brian's loss, we returned to our daily routine of going to work and attending school in the best way we could. After Brian, it would never be the same.

On a cold afternoon in mid-February, I was looking out the window watching the snow fall. It was quiet and peaceful. I stared at the top of the tall pine trees wondering what it would be like to view the snowy scene from a mountaintop. I decided to bundle up and enjoy the beauty of the moment.

While looking for my boots in our guest bedroom closet, I came across a cardboard box that had "Mom and Dad" scribbled across its side. It was written in haste, no doubt, by one of the kids. Upon closer inspection, I realized it was Brian's handwriting. My heart leaped, and I fell to my knees, sobbing.

Through my tears, I could see that there were gifts for all of us, including Christmas cards. I opened one of the boxes, and there was a set of beautiful wine glasses, with a note tucked inside that read: "Mom, Dad, Celebrate every day. Love, Brian."

I knew what he meant—he would always be with us. I clutched the note to my chest, forever grateful for having such a wonderful son. I realized that the passage of time and strong faith would help to heal our grieving hearts.

The following day, I bought Valentine's Day cards for my husband and children, expressing my love and gratitude for them. We came together and celebrated our love and appreciation for one another. We finally opened our gifts and thanked God for one another and for the special time we had for 19 years with Brian.

Yvonne E. Lancaster is a former newspaper columnist and the recipient of numerous writing awards from United Press International, Massachusetts Press Association, and New England Press Association for her column *From the Heart*. Currently, she writes short stories and poetry, and is a still-life painter. She is co-author of *Every Step of the Way: How Four Mothers Coped with Child Loss* and *From the Heart, Sketches from Life*. She was named Woman of the Year by the Business and Professional Women of America. Find more articles by Yvonne at www.opentohope.com.

Grieving Through the Holidays: Changing Expectations

By Catherine Tidd

I know I'm not the only one who is feeling the effects of the season.

Grieving during "normal" times is a full-time job. Throw in two or three holidays back-to-back and whatever milestones we might have in the middle and, well, we're all working on nervous breakdowns of epic proportions.

I think one of the cruelest things about the holidays (and this may just be me) is that we're dealing with something that we used to look forward to so much, and it's turned into something we can barely get through.

My first Christmas without my husband was definitely the hardest. That should come as no surprise. It came about four months after his death, and the truth is, I was still in such a fog that I really hadn't given much thought to how exactly I would get through it. (That worry came the second year, when I was actually "with it" enough to worry.)

To tell you the truth, memories of that first Christmas are just now starting to resurface. Everything was so crazy at that point, I really don't remember much. That first Christmas came at the peak of my "manic" phase. I was running around like the Tasmanian devil, and then I completely crashed that February.

That was my first valuable Grief Lesson: You can't outrun it. It's within you and will find its way out somehow.

I couldn't sit still. I didn't want to think about what had happened or exactly how I was going to make this new life work. I think I was actually too crazy for therapy at that point.

Yikes.

I was delusional enough that I had completely tricked myself into thinking I was the same person I had always been. I wanted to assure everyone around me that nothing had changed. You don't have to be uncomfortable around me! Sure, our family is missing one person, but heck, we can do this! I don't need anyone to feel sorry for us. We're fine!

The folks from Webster's Dictionary called recently and asked if they could put my 2007 picture next the word "denial." I told them no. That really wasn't my best hair year.

As I was getting ready to decorate my house this year, feeling a little less overwhelmed and a little more hopeful than I have in Christmases past, I asked my sister, "Do you remember that first Christmas and that party I gave? Was I crazy or what?"

"Yup. You pretty much were."

Don't ask a question you don't want to know the answer to.

I got it into my head, somewhere around the middle of November, that I was going to have a party. None of this widow stuff for me! I was going to invite over every single person I knew and throw a shindig like they had never seen before.

Not only that, but I decided to invite over people I knew who sell stuff. I had a different vendor in every room of the main floor of my house. Pampered Chef in the kitchen, jewelry in the living room, purses in the TV room, and chocolate in the dining room. If I could have figured out someone appropriate for the bathroom, I would have booked him.

I decorated every square inch. When I ran out of decorations, I bought more. Greenery on every surface I could think of. White lights *everywhere*. I didn't stop until it looked like Christmas threw up in my house.

Of course, manic decorating has to end at some point. The guests come, and then they leave. And then I was stuck with a whole bunch of Christmas cheer and no one to share it with.

Kind of made me want to torch the whole thing.

Now, this story may strike some as odd. Most people suffering a loss can't rouse themselves out of their grief-induced stupor to even put up any decorations. And I get that. That was year two for me. (I've already told you guys I'm a weird griever.)

Coming up on Christmas number four, I think I've figured a few things out. I have had to reverse my thinking about this time of year. Instead of expecting to whoop it up at a bunch of parties and see every single person from my past within a two-week time period, I'm looking forward to just being in my house with my Netflix subscription and endless cups of hot tea.

Instead of trying to hit every Christmas program I can find, I've told my kids to choose one, and we'll make an event out of it. Instead of expecting myself to jolly everyone else along for the next few weeks, I'll celebrate the fact that I'm just getting through it.

This year, I've learned to say "No" a little more and commit myself to less, so I don't feel quite so overwhelmed and exhausted.

I've learned to change my expectations a little—just temporarily. There comes a point when you have to realize that you can't completely recreate the magic of Christmases past.

Actually, you've probably already had to make that kind of transition before. Holidays as an adult are really not the same as they are as a child.

Over the years, you've had to change how you celebrate and make your own magic. When you got married, you had to blend your traditions together to create something new. If you have children, you had to change again, from letting the wine flow on Christmas Eve to drinking coffee so you didn't completely screw up Barbie's Dreamhouse. And now that you've lost your partner in crime, those traditions have to be changed yet again.

But coming from someone who is working her way into a new life she wasn't expecting, I've learned that it *will* get better. There is still joy to be had. Miracles still find a way into our lives. At some point, the lights will twinkle again and you'll find yourself gazing at a house with really hideous decorations, with a little grin on your face.

If you hit your manic phase later than I did, be aware: It could be *your* house.

Catherine Tidd is a widow and the founder of a free social support network dedicated to anyone who has lost a significant other. She is also a writer, public speaker, and mother to three young, entertaining children. She earned her English degree from Rollins College in 1998 and lives in Denver, CO. To read more of her work, visit www.opentohope.com.

A Sign of Hope from Mom

By Megan Prescott

In 1987, when I was 18 years old, my mother was diagnosed with an aggressive form of leukemia two weeks before Christmas. My dad, brother, and I brought the holiday into her hospital room that year in the midst of her chemotherapy, opening a few presents and watching her struggle to have a bite or two of the homemade turkey dinner. What I couldn't have imagined then was that in eight short months my mother, Nancy, would pass, to be followed a mere three weeks later by my brother, Adam, from a violent car accident.

In the months that followed, I thought a lot about a specific conversation I had had with my mother a few days before her death. "If you go to the other side," I asked, "will you give me a sign?"

With a faint and tired smile she replied, "A sign? Like what?"

"A feather," I said, "any color."

Just a few months after the deaths of my mother and brother, Christmas came back around. It was hard to comprehend that only one year earlier my family had been intact. But now, it absolutely wasn't. Rather than ignoring the holiday like I wanted to, I decided to try and focus on the spirit of the season and just get through it.

That Christmas Eve, I attended a midnight mass service, after much prompting from a friend. Christmas was the only day of the year that my mom insisted I go to church with her. The thought of going without her that year was devastating. But I knew it was a concrete way to honor her, and she would be pleased if I continued on with the tradition. And so with a heavy heart, I went.

Up and down, kneel and stand, stand and kneel, the Christmas service was nearly halfway through. As instructed by the priest, I knelt once more right before beginning the Lord's Prayer, a favorite of my mother's. As I knelt down, I saw something amazing. Lying right in front of me was a large white and gray feather! I was stunned.

How did this feather appear in front of me when it hadn't been there moments before? Had I missed it? No, not possible. I tapped the shoulder of the man in the pew in front of me and asked if the feather was his—and even if he had chickens! I still remember his confused look as he shook his head no.

Then I remembered my conversation with my mom and my request for a feather. She was giving me the sign that she was safe and okay! In that moment, I felt like I had been touched by an angel. I knew that even though I couldn't see her anymore with my physical eyes, my mom wasn't gone from me completely. I understood she was letting me know that she was "alive" and still somehow with me; not even death could separate us. This feather was a miraculous gift to me from my mother.

Since that day, there have been numerous signs and dreams that have convinced me that both my mother and brother are still very connected to my life, even more than two decades later.

To anyone who has had to say good-bye to someone they love, I dedicate this story. May you be reminded that miracles and magic happen every day, especially now during the season of light.

The only thing you have to do to experience a miracle is simply ask for one.

Megan Prescott has used words and images to document her own bereavement journey for over 20 years. At age 19, Megan experienced the death of both her mother and brother within a month of each other. Since then, she has brought the healing power of the arts to schools, shelters, grieving families, and herself. Megan is an artist, teacher, and author of *Squirrel and Oak: A Story of Hope*. For more information, please visit www.opentohope.com.

I'll Take a Christmas Tree, Stocking, and Tissues for the Road

By Kathryn McGrath

The halls are decked out with glittered things galore, our stockings are hung on the mantle with care, and our Christmas tree is trimmed to the top because of an unexpected amount of holiday cheer. I couldn't ask for anything more.

Oh wait. Yes, I could. Dear Brother, where are you? If only you could be here this very second!

Indeed, I find it funny how the holiday season can be like this. At one point, I can find myself totally calm and in a state of complete bliss, especially after hearing my favorite piano rendition of "What Child Is This?" But then it hits me, something is triggered internally and, boy, am I bitter!

Whenever I decorate for Christmas I find myself merry and full of holiday cheer at one moment, and then—SNAP! The tears begin flowing. If I had a tissue for every time that happened! In a store, for example, I might see Christmas cards for "Brothers" or "Sisters." The design and layout of the cards are lovely, which is something I can appreciate; the fact that I cannot give or receive such cards anymore is what brings up feelings of sadness.

How odd it is—yet how awesome, too—to go from one end of the emotional spectrum to the other in a matter of seconds. The human mind must be quite something if it can, at one and the same time, think in the present and in the past.

Around this time of year, I often think about how I would give anything to spend a moment with my brother, to wish him a "Merry Christmas!" and "Happy New Year!" directly, face-to-face. As wonderful as that might be, I also think of the many experiences I have had since his death, moments that I doubt would have happened had he survived. It seems grief is quite a paradox. After all, it is the price one pays for loving another.

To have only the joyful emotions running through me would be fantastic. So, too, would the chance to see once again those I love who have died, particularly my sibling. Since that cannot happen, I will take both—the happy and the sad.

Likewise, I will welcome the fact that, on one hand, I love Christmas and all I associate with it. Those associations, however, can also cause quite a stir within me. So, I will understand why I have so much angst this time of year, rather than guilt myself away from those raw and bitter feelings. I will appreciate the Christmas trees, stockings, and gifts galore, but I will also acknowledge the softness and comfort a tissue can bring, and I will take one for the road.

On second thought, make that a box of tissues!

Kathryn McGrath comes from New England, where in 2008 she earned a B.A. in theology from Saint Anselm College in Manchester, NH, after which she completed a Master's degree in Pastoral Ministry from the Boston College School of Theology and Ministry in Chestnut Hill, MA. Kathryn is pursuing a Master's degree in Mental Health Counseling at Rivier College in Nashua, NH. Her general interests include the integration of theology and psychology. Read more by Kathryn at www.opentohope.com.

Even This Santa Gives Thanks

By Nan Zastrow

The hustle and bustle of the holiday season begins. Shopping carts are brimming with purchases. Early in the season, there is a sense of joy. It's the miraculous part of Christmas, when good moods prevail and everyone is wrapped up in the joyous preparation. We become Santa as we plan the perfect holiday celebration.

I once played the role of Santa, too. Today, there is something missing from the Santa scene.

Since our first Christmas without my son, Chad, I've never been quite as enthusiastic about the holiday as I once was. There is an overriding sense of pain that hangs over the merriment that others feel. It stifles the comfort of music, takes the fun out of tradition, and dulls many memories that once sparkled. Grief and Ebenezer Scrooge make good bedfellows. I soon realized the center of our holiday was our loved ones. Chad was the special element that put "thankfulness" into Thanksgiving, "happy" into Birthday, and "merry" into Christmas.

Playing Santa for him was always a challenge. He could produce a list 16 pages long without much effort. And he would smile mischievously at his accomplishment. Whatever I ended up buying was still a surprise! But more than the gifts were the good times: The piñatas and Santa visits as children; the hidden presents and other traditions as adults. Santa lived in our hearts.

That first holiday after his death, my heart ached with every thought of celebration. I tried all the tips for coping, but nothing seemed right. I even talked to my family early on about "changing our traditions"—doing things differently. I remember, clearly, sitting on the golf course in August, with my sister, wanting advice about how our family was going to cope. It's no wonder that by the time the holidays arrived my anxiety level had peaked. All I wanted to do was get it over with!

I didn't make a very good Santa that year. I couldn't have cared less if I shopped. It hurt to watch the children. I couldn't find peace in the religious celebrations. I cried over every ornament I hung on the tree. I backed out of Christmas Eve services. And, as much as I tried to make things normal for everyone else, I couldn't find a bit of peace for myself. I was a Santa with no reason to be jolly.

I was miserable by choice. I was angry at God for allowing my life to take such a turn. I felt sorry for myself and wanted everyone to feel my pain. I couldn't deny it. It's easy to give thanks when life is splendid. But giving thanks when you face dark moments is a priceless message of trust.

For a brief time every year, the nagging pain of Christmases-past beckons at my door, reminding me of where I've been and where I am today. Today, with certainty, I can say, "Facing the holidays is easier, but it's very different."

In the darkness of this journey through grief, there are some shining lights. The gifts I've received aren't from Santa, but they are blessings:

- I am blessed to know that my God is always with me. No matter what I felt or what I said in His presence, He understood. And even today, when I have memory lapses and pity myself, He is there for me. What a friend I have in Jesus!
- I am blessed because I can choose my attitude, and my choices give me new options. I still miss the things I'll never have, but I don't ponder them anymore.
- I am blessed with family and friends who value my commitments and support me beyond a shadow of a doubt. This gives value to what I do.
- I am blessed because God has given me the gift of writing, and I've found a way to use this gift to soothe the pain.
- I am blessed with a healthy mind, body, and spirit, even though I sometimes take them for granted.
- I am blessed with the gift of purpose each morning. I like the quote: "God put me on this earth to accomplish a certain number of things. Right now I'm so far behind, I will never die!"

I purchased a figurine of Santa on bended knee, head bowed, arms folded. It reminds me of those early years of holiday grief. Perhaps the craftsman's interpretation was meant to capture the magic of Santa and the miracle of Christmas that brings two stories together to serve a higher purpose. Or maybe it was Santa giving thanks after his arduous task of delivering packages. Or maybe he was just thankful that the holiday was finally over this year!

Life is a gift. For my son, Chad, the gift of life was brief. But in the brevity of those 21 years, he lived and touched the lives of many. Most of all, he touched mine. His death uncovered my weaknesses, but the spirit of his being has brought out the music in my soul.

I remind myself that it's okay to yearn for the past, but only momentarily. There is much to do in the present. Our tree sparkles with ornaments that tell the stories of many beautiful Christmases-past. Ornaments remind me of family members who have died. There are messages in sparkling angels, stars of hope, and bells of joy. And, always the silent chorus of beautiful memories. With all this to be grateful for, even this Santa can give thanks!

After the loss of their son in 1993, Nan and Gary Zastrow created a ministry of hope through their non-profit organization. Writing became Nan's outlet for expressing her feelings. Nan writes about her transforming grief journey and offers hope to others through her words. She is the author of four books and over 60 articles in magazines and Internet grief sites. Nan and Gary have full-time careers, in addition to countless volunteer hours dedicated to helping the bereaved. Learn more by visiting www.opentohope.com.

Advice for Suicide Loss Survivors

By Catherine Greenleaf

As suicide loss survivors, we often dread the holiday season. Christmas music tells us to be jolly, but sometimes our grief is too heavy and we just can't work up the enthusiasm. However, by giving ourselves permission to take care of ourselves, we can take control and feel self-empowered—regardless of what the relatives may say. Here are some tips to help you along:

Tip #1: The most important thing you can do this holiday season, or at any time, is to put yourself with safe people who validate your loss.

Tip #2: Don't feel you have to accept every holiday party invitation you receive. Pick and choose.

Tip #3: Have a Plan B. If you go to a party and someone upsets you, have a phone number handy of someone you can call for support.

Tip #4: Be sure to plan quiet time at home alone for yourself during the holidays, so you can enjoy some peace of mind.

Tip #5: Be a chipper! To make life more manageable,

steadily chip away at your holiday gift list. Instead of attempting to buy all your gifts in one trip to the mall, chunk it down into several smaller trips. This will help you avoid the last-minute rush.

Tip #6: Use the Internet or mail-order catalogs to shop if driving to busy stores or malls unnerves you.

Tip #7: Try to make wrapping gifts a pleasant experience. Put on the holiday music, make yourself a cup of cocoa, eat a candy cane, and wrap.

Tip #8: As with any activity, if you feel overwhelmed, put everything away for another day.

Tip #9: The temptation to overindulge will be great. Keep in mind that alcohol is a depressant. Too much sugar can make some people emotional and even weepy. Dark chocolate sweets can keep some people awake all night.

Tip #10: The average American can gain 5-10 pounds over the course of the holiday season, which can be very depressing. Moderation is key. Eat before you arrive so you won't nibble all night. Find interesting people to take your mind off food.

Tip #11: If family relations are contentious, put time limits on how long you will visit. You can craft a high-quality holiday with family by limiting your visit to five hours. After five hours, put on your coat and get out.

Tip #12: Remember the Holiday Golden Hour—that first hour of any holiday gathering. It's the safest time to be there. After several hours, drinkers start to get drunk and obnoxious, kids get whiny and cranky, and relatives start making sarcastic remarks. Give yourself permission to leave any situation you find stressful or unsettling.

Catherine Greenleaf is a non-denominational spiritual counselor and longtime member of the Association for Death Education and Counseling. She is the author of the highly acclaimed book *Healing the Hurt Spirit: Daily Affirmations for People Who Have Lost a Loved One to Suicide* and the positive affirmation CD *Today, I Am Healing.* Catherine is a suicide loss survivor who has lost three people to suicide. She travels nationwide to share the story of her own healing and how it is possible to survive suicide loss. Find more articles by Catherine at www.opentohope.com.

Michael's Gift to Me: Feeling the Zing

By Ron Villano, MS, LMHC, ASAC, CCH

I just purchased my third Christmas tree since I lost my son, Michael, in 1998. I've got to admit, this year I felt a little blue and a bit uncaring about the holiday celebrations. I spent some time acknowledging that I miss my son. I also miss my mom, dad, brother-in-law, and others who are no longer here.

And while it would seem that this would be the obvious cause of my blues, I found that it was only a small piece of a larger puzzle.

Since I was still lacking that special ho ho ho, I began to check into other factors—relationships, things to do, stress, and the like. I found some issues there, too, and took time to address them. It helped lift some more weight. But I still felt something missing.

So then I took my own Zing advice and did a quick check in my mind's Garage. Ah ha! Found something that was bothering me. It amazes even me that things still tend to get dumped in there when I stop paying attention. I talked with my favorite Light Bulb people and took care of that piece of this holiday puzzle.

And then I did what everyone should do during the holiday season. I sat down for less than 15 minutes and made a list of all the things I was thankful for in my life then and now. This was Michael's gift to me this year. How? I learned how to live a whole new life because I lived through the loss of my 17-year-old son over 12 years ago.

Yes, I felt the Zing inside once again.

It's not about what you don't have during the holidays. It's about what you need to let go of during this season of hustle and bustle. And when you can make room in your mind, you will find that the craziness of the season settles down, and the spirit of giving, loving, and living life will rise and carry you right into the New Year.

Do someZing amaZing this holiday season. Make sure you take time to check your mind's Garage, talk with your favorite Light Bulbs, and create a little peace and joy in your own heart, mind, and soul.

Blessings to you for a peaceful and joyous holiday!

Ron Villano, MS, LMHC, ASAC, CCH, is a leading expert on change. As a bereaved father, he speaks from the heart. As a licensed psychotherapist, he counsels others on working through difficult times. As a nationally recognized speaker and author, Ron appears before sold-out audiences across the country. His fun, captivating, and approachable style creates the powerful, life-changing moments you have been looking for. Read his articles at www.opentohope.com.

PART 4

Embracing the New Year with Hope

How Were the Holidays for You?

By Mitch Carmody

Christmas is over. Thank God for small miracles. When you have suffered the physical loss of someone in your life, the holidays, especially Christmas, can be extremely difficult and challenging. When that loss is a child, it can change how you experience and process the holidays forever.

As many bereaved know, our grief journey soon becomes a subversive, evocative *it*, an acceptable pronoun to minimize the reality of a condition that no *fortunate other* can comprehend nor wants to imagine—the loss of a child in their family. So the world and we tend to hush it up, whisper our pain, and not talk about *it*. We don our dancing shoes and tap dance for the world to music we have come to loathe. "Joy to the World." Yeah, right. Hop in my sleigh and go for a ride.

It starts, however, long before Christmas and endures through the New Year's festivities. How do I cook and baste a turkey with love when my cup is empty? How can I *not shop* for the loved one who so loved my Christmas presents? How do I feel thankful when I feel so cheated? How do I manufacture Christmas cheer? How do I hold in the agony I experience when other parents hug and snuggle their children? How do we do *it*?

We do *it* because *it* is our kids. *It* is our grief. *It* is not a condition or a stage we go through; *it* is picking up our shattered lives. We are in a process of transmogrification as surely as a caterpillar creates a cocoon. Sometime in the future, the chrysalis wrapped around our injured souls will become clear as does the caterpillar's, and we will know that it is our time to rejoin the world, which takes as long as it takes

We are changed forever, but we can find joy again…as elusive as it may seem. We can choose to become more collateral damage to our loss or we can strive to be intentional survivors in this world—a world in which we experience our intended destiny. It's a journey we were meant to discover, despite its dark despair. Our children have angel wings; we have butterfly wings. Together, we can soar as one in our hearts until we too get our own angel wings and soar into eternity. They are now our teachers, and we are now the students. It's ass backward, I know, but it is what it is.

I buried my child with his body in those early years; this did not work for me. The world became an emotional desert painted in different shades of gray. I wanted color back, I wanted the beach back, I wanted the smell of spring lilacs back, I wanted my son back. So I returned to the pain; I returned to the facts. I started grieving for him all over again.

I dived back into my grief headlong, bringing my son's name back to life in this world, making him an active participant not only in my life, but in the lives of others. Why did no one give me permission to do this? Why did everyone accept the finality of his death without compunction, resistance, or retort?

Like silent lambs to the slaughter, we sometimes accept society's dictates on how to process loss, and we move on as urged and expected. We become complacent because we have no strength or there seem to be no real alternatives. Life sucks, and we accept the fact it always will, and we move on and get over it. That siren of apathy charted my course for many years, and life was lusterless and listless.

When I started getting signs from my son, Kelly, they broke the siren's spell, and we started a new relationship on a nonphysical level. I brought Kelly back into my life with my book, my speaking, and my everyday living. Like the movie *Pleasantville,* my black-and-white world turned back to color. Wow! Not only did I discover that there is life after death for my son, I realized it was true for me as well.

My grief, no longer a noun, has become an action verb. We live our loss with action, with intent, and with anticipation, and we celebrate the rest of our lives *with* our children, not without them. We just say *no* to those who tell us we must move on and how we should be over *it*. There is no getting over *it*. *It* is me! Deal with me. What you see is what you get, and *it* ain't going away.

Christmases will come and go, and you will always have that nagging feeling that you have forgotten something, or feel you are waiting for the package that never arrives. Those feelings do not go away, but color can come back to Christmas and into your life someday...if you believe.

Mitch Carmody's 9-year-old son died of cancer in 1987. He published *Letters to My Son: A Journey Through Grief* and now lectures and conducts grief workshops nationally for The Compassionate Friends and Bereaved Parents USA, in addition to writing articles for many national bereavement periodicals. Mitch is a trained hospice volunteer. He lives in rural Minnesota with his wife. Read more articles by Mitch at www.opentohope.com.

Many New Year's Eves Later?

By Katy Hutchison

December 31st has come and gone many times since my husband, Bob, was murdered. While ringing in the New Year with friends, Bob left our dinner table to check on the home of a vacationing neighbor. It had become apparent that no responsible adult was overseeing a party that the neighbor's teenage son was throwing. Bob walked in on about two hundred drunk and out-of-control youth. Within minutes, he was dead, beaten to death by two young men angered by his efforts to shut things down. I was left a widow with 4-year-old twins.

The first year after Bob's death was a blur of just getting one foot in front of the other. I focused my energy on putting meals on the table for my children, easing them into the routine of kindergarten, and crying myself to sleep.

Having the anniversary of Bob's death fall on a holiday magnified the dread I felt as the first Christmas season approached. I made arrangements to take my children away that first year, something we had never done before. Just the thought of snow, the familiar boxes of decorations, the smell of turkey, and one less place set at our table made me want to fall off the edge of the earth.

We spent the holidays on a beach in Mexico. My children were kept busy by the impossibly happy recreation staff while I hid my swollen eyes behind sunglasses and pretended to read a trashy novel. While the rest of the resort gaily counted down the minutes to midnight, I pulled the covers over my head and prayed the next year would be easier.

The next year was not any easier, but it was different. I had remarried and my husband, Michael, had two children of his own. We made a real effort to create new holiday traditions that would honor our freshly blended family. I began a different repertoire of Christmas baking and laid to rest some of Bob's favorites.

Michael's daughter is biracial. Her beautiful almond-shaped eyes and shiny black hair show off her Asian heritage, and it was her suggestion to celebrate Chinese New Year. We held off popping the champagne in December, and ate duck and oranges in February instead. I still felt myself bracing for the holidays weeks in advance, but the jagged edges were smoothed somewhat by the curiosity of discovering new rituals.

In the years that followed, my sadness was more about how much of the children's lives Bob was missing. Our twins had grown into adolescence and offered reminders of Bob's character with ever-increasing frequency. The arrival of each New Year simply served to remind me of his absence in our world.

I learned to be good to myself as the holidays approached—not overcommitting the family socially and building in lots of time and space to look after one another's hearts. I made a habit of going to bed before the ball dropped.

A few years ago on December 31st, I found our kitchen crowded with an impromptu gathering of friends and family. A close friend's marriage had just fallen apart, and she had brought her children along to get away from her own holiday grief.

I realized that night that life does move forward. It brings with it new circumstances to celebrate, as well as new circumstances to mourn. I was grateful my grief for Bob had shrunk enough to allow room in my heart to help my friend get through her own loss. Before I knew it, it was midnight—the first time in many years I had seen the New Year in. My arms encircled my friend on one side and Michael on the other. Our children danced with sparklers on the lawn while our tears of joy flowed amidst tears of sadness. Life *and* death are messy.

Now our twins are in their teens, and New Year's Eve has become an exciting social event among their peers. They confessed to me a concern that I would never let them go out to celebrate. On the contrary, I am grateful for their healthy, normal, and very typical teen need to be with their friends. I explained to them they have a lifetime of New Year's Eves ahead of them. They deserve to look forward to that night with eager anticipation, for it to be special and enjoyed safely in the company of good people. They deserve it to be the start of something wonderful rather than a reminder of a horrible moment in time. Bob would be the first to agree.

Gung Hay Fat Choy!

Katy Hutchison, the mother of 18-year-old twins, Emma and Sam, resides with her family in Victoria, BC. After the horrific murder of her husband, Bob, on New Year's Eve 1997, Katy waited for five years while the police worked tirelessly to obtain the evidence to prosecute and convict his killers. She is the author of *Walking After Midnight: One Woman's Journey Through Murder, Justice and Forgiveness*. Read more articles at www.opentohope.com.

How to Avoid Carrying the Burden of Guilt into the New Year

By Marty Tousley

We often feel guilty for what we did or didn't do, said or failed to say, when our loved one was alive, even if there is no basis in reality for these feelings. In fact, this feeling of guilt in the aftermath of significant loss is so common, it's almost universal.

The beginning of a New Year is a good time to confront that guilt, understand it, release it, and move forward with good intentions.

Guilt is a normal response to the perception that we've somehow failed in our duties and obligations, or that we've done something wrong. It generates a whole mixture of feelings, including doubt, shame, inadequacy, insecurity, failure, unworthiness, self-judgment and blame, anxiety, and fear of punishment.

Some authors make the distinction between guilt and regret, noting that guilt is the feeling we have when our conscience is violated, while regret is the feeling of sadness that results when things don't turn out the way we had hoped. Guilt implies that we are at fault for something we've done or failed to do; regret is a reflection of our humanness.

As imperfect human beings, we are limited in our capacities—after all, there is only so much anyone can do in the face of insurmountable odds. We cannot be held accountable for circumstances beyond our control or for consequences we cannot foresee. At some point, we must find a way to forgive ourselves for our human imperfections.

When your loved one's terminal illness was finally diagnosed, you may have felt guilty that you hadn't noticed the symptoms sooner, waited too long to seek treatment, or didn't do enough to comfort him or her. If death came suddenly or unexpectedly, you may feel guilty for not being present when it happened. If it came after a long, lingering illness, you may feel guilty for feeling relieved that your loved one's suffering is over and you're now free from the burden of worry and care. You may feel guilty that you are the one who survived or uncomfortable that you received an insurance settlement or inheritance following the death of your loved one. If you're a religious person, you may feel guilty that you feel so angry at God.

Unfortunately, guilt is a natural and common component of grief. When someone you love dies, it's only human to search for an explanation, to look at what you did or did not do, and to dwell on the *what ifs* and *if onlys*. You agonize and tell yourself, "If only I'd done something differently, this never would've happened."

Sometimes, though, there simply isn't anything you could have done differently. When your loved one's illness or death occurred, chances are that whatever happened beforehand was not intentional on your part. Given the stress you were under then and how exhausted you may have been, you were doing the best you could. Given the information available to you at the time, you were doing what you normally would have done.

Harsh as it may seem, consider that even if you had done things differently, your loved one still may have died in some other way, at some other time. Sometimes we act as if we can control the random hazards of existence, even when we know that death is a fact of life.

Guilt is driven by our own personal beliefs and expectations, and dealing with it requires that we examine what we think we did wrong, face it, and evaluate it as objectively as possible. For example, what did you expect of yourself that you did not live up to? Were your expectations unrealistic? If they were, then you need to let go of them. Since you did all that you were capable of doing at the time, there simply is no basis for your guilt, and you need to let go of that as well.

Nevertheless, if after careful examination of the facts, you find that your expectations of yourself are legitimate and you still did not live up to them, it's important to face and take responsibility for what you believe you could have done differently. Healthy guilt allows us to own up to and learn from our mistakes. It gives us a chance to make amends, to do things differently next time, to come to a better understanding of ourselves, and to forgive ourselves and move on.

Tips for Coping with Guilt

- Identify what it is that you feel guilty about. Resist the urge to keep such thoughts and feelings to yourself like so many deep, dark secrets. Bring them out into the open where they can be examined.

Share them with a trusted friend or counselor, who can view your thoughts and feelings more objectively and challenge what may be irrational or illogical.

- Listen to the messages you give yourself (the should haves, could haves, and if onlys), and realize the past is something you can do absolutely nothing about.
- When guilty thoughts come to mind, disrupt them by telling yourself to stop thinking such thoughts. Say *"Stop!"* firmly—out loud if you need to.
- Live the next day or next week of your life as if you were guilt-free, knowing you can return to your guilt feelings any time you wish. Pick a start time and stop yourself whenever you make any guilt-related statements to yourself or anyone else.
- Write down your guilt-related statements, set a date, and pledge that from that day forward, you won't say them to yourself anymore. Post them and read them every day.
- If you are troubled by feeling relieved that your loved one's suffering has ended, know that a heavy burden has been lifted from your shoulders. You have been released from an emotionally exhausting and physically draining experience, and to feel relieved is certainly understandable.
- If you believe in God or a higher power, consider what He or She has to say about forgiveness.
- Participate in a support group. It's a powerful way to obtain forgiveness and absolution from others.
- Be your own best friend. What would you have

said to your best friend if this had happened to that person? Can you say the same to yourself?

- Remember the good things you did in your relationship with your loved one and all the loving care you gave. Focus on the positive aspects—what you learned from each other, what you did together that brought you joy, laughter, and excitement. Write those things down and read them whenever you need to.
- Ask what you expected of yourself that you didn't live up to. How is it that you didn't? What were the circumstances at the time? What have you learned from this that you'll do differently next time?
- What can you do to make amends? Find a way to genuinely apologize to your loved one's spirit and ask for forgiveness.
- Have a visit with your loved one. Say aloud or in your mind whatever you didn't get to say while he or she was still living. Be as honest as you can be.
- If your loved one were writing a letter to you, what would this person say to you about the guilt and sadness you've been carrying around?
- Ask what it would take for you to forgive yourself. Can you begin doing it? Say out loud to yourself, "I forgive you." Say it several times a day.
- Remember that no one else can absolve your feelings of guilt—only you can do so, through the process of intentionally forgiving yourself.
- When you've consciously learned all you can learn

from this situation, and when you've made any amends you consider necessary, then it's time to let go of your guilt, forgive yourself, and move on.

- Channel the energy of your guilt into a worthwhile project. Do good deeds in your loved one's honor.

Having experienced many losses herself, including the unexpected death of an infant, Marty Tousley found her calling as a grief counselor with Hospice of the Valley in Phoenix, AZ, and serves as moderator for its online Grief Healing Discussion Groups. She has authored several publications addressing various aspects of loss and grief, including *Finding Your Way through Grief: A Guide for the First Year*. Read more articles by Marty at www.opentohope.com.

Steering Toward Happiness

By Christine Thiele

Every New Year, I try to sit down, evaluate progress and failure, and write a message of hope for myself, my family, and others. This year, as far as I've come in the five-plus years since my husband's death, I still feel I have twice as far to go.

I've moved from barely breathing to surviving. I hope my next step will be to thrive again.

In those early days, the fog was thick, tears flowed continuously, and my heart was hopeless. Now, my tears are triggered less often, my mind is clear again, and I have a working plan toward a future I never anticipated. I know my heart has hope within it again because I am able, and some days even willing, to look toward the future.

Early on, a woman in one of my support groups said something that has resonated with me for years. "There's nothing to look forward to." Those six little words summed up our lives at that point. For many years, I have felt this way.

That lovely woman became one of my most treasured travel companions on the widow journey. We have both struggled to come up with our Plan Bs, and then our Plan Cs. We have tried new jobs, new homes, and new support systems, and, somehow, we landed on our feet. Somehow, the choices we have made since our spouses died have carried us through this awful journey of lost love and grief. We're never sure if our new plans will work, but when they do, I know I discover a new piece of hope or rediscover a part of me that has been hiding in the shadows of grief.

As far as I've come, I have that much farther to travel on this path. My planning came from the need to provide for my family financially. I have again become a chameleon, changing the scenarios around me to provide the basic needs—housing, food, safety—as I also work to preserve the needs that I see as a priority in my children's daily lives.

So, now that I've got the scaffolding in place, I need to build the ongoing support and extras that make a life joyful. How can I be a more loving person when I am so afraid of losing love again? How can I invest further in my relationships with those around me when my gut wants me to build protective walls, gates, and security for my heart, instead of doors and windows that let love and joy into my life?

It is not an easy task. I believe that this ability to risk and be joyful again is the key to my ongoing healing. I believe that I will be more able to handle all the stresses in my life as a sole parent when I can allow and really give myself permission to be happy again. I keep happiness at arm's length now, because maybe if I'm happy, I've somehow lost my husband in another way?

This New Year, I hope to let the controls go a little and perhaps steer into happiness. Maybe the roads of this journey will change and lead me to a place where I can balance my grief with happiness, really thriving instead of just getting through the days.

My wish for all those reading this is that your hearts will be lighter, and joy and abundance will fill your life in the year to come.

Happy New Year!

Christine Thiele is a freelance writer. She has written for *The Journal of Student Ministries, YouthWorker Journal,* and *Grief Digest*. Since her husband's death, her writing is focused on grief and healing issues. Her blog, *Memoirs from Widow Island: A Journey Toward Healing,* chronicles her life as a widow striving toward healing and hope. Along with her writing, Christine is raising two young sons. Read more at www.opentohope.com.

About the Authors

Dr. Gloria C. Horsley, PhD, MFC, RN, and Dr. Heidi Horsley, PsyD, LMSW, MS, are internationally recognized grief experts. This mother/daughter team founded the Open to Hope Foundation and are hosts of the "Open to Hope" Internet radio show. In addition, Dr. Gloria is a former Board Member for The Compassionate Friends. Dr. Heidi currently serves on The Compassionate Friends Board and the Tragedy Assistance Program for Survivors Advisory Board. Dr. Heidi is also an adjunct professor at Columbia University, with a private practice in Manhattan. Together, they have written a number of articles and several books, including *Open to Hope: Inspirational Stories of Healing After Loss,* which they coauthored with the Open to Hope Contributors; *Teen Grief Relief*; and the award-winning *Real Men Do Cry,* which they coauthored with Eric Hipple. Dr. Gloria also wrote *The In-Law Survival Guide.* Find more at www.opentohope.com.

Dr. Gloria and Dr. Heidi are deeply indebted to the authors who graciously shared their journeys through holiday grief in this book and the many more on the Open to Hope website, www.opentohope.com.